# GARDEN PONDS

Garden Ponds are now so easy to construct using modern fibre glass materials, concrete or plastic, that they come well within the scope of the enthusiastic amateur. Even the smallest garden can now be graced by a pond in which the owner can raise his own fish or grow his own aquatic plants.

This book will show you how to build a pond in a short time, and tell you what to put in it.

# GARDEN PONDS

by

ARTHUR BOARDER

FOYLES HANDBOOKS
LONDON

*ISBN 0 7071 0606 0*

*First published 1967*
*Reprinted 1969*
*Reprinted 1970*
*Reprinted 1971*
*Reprinted 1973*
*Revised edition 1977*
*Reprinted 1980*
*Reprinted 1982*
*Reprinted 1984*

*© W. & G. Foyle Ltd. 1967*

*Published in Great Britain by*
*W. & G. Foyle Ltd.,*
*125 Charing Cross Road,*
*London, WC2H 0EB*

*Printed and bound in Great Britain*
*at The Pitman Press, Bath*

## CONTENTS

## ILLUSTRATIONS

# GARDEN PONDS

F EW GARDENS could be deemed complete without a
pond, as the sight of water and perhaps the trickling
of a water-fall or fountain give an added attraction at all
times. There is something peaceful about the sound of
water especially on a hot day when one is relaxing on the
lawn in a deck-chair. A well sited and constructed pond
can give that extra finish to an ornamental garden that
will immediately set it above any ordinary garden which
has no pond. There are other features about such a pond
which can increase the attraction to many people. Beautiful water lilies can be grown and flowered with practically
no trouble at all and many other handsome water plants
can be grown to add to the floral scene.

Another interest for the pond-keeper is that fishes can be
bred in the pond to give a fascinating hobby which con-
tinues throughout the years as the spawning of the fishes,
hatching and growing of the youngsters, is an unending
source of interest. Once the pond is made there is little
trouble to be taken to keep everything running smoothly.
One important point is that no matter how long a drought
lasts there will be no need to water the lilies and other
flowering plants in the pond. A well balanced pond will
need very little attention and will give less work to look
after than any other part of the garden.

Some people are afraid that a pond in the garden will attract mosquitoes and gnats, but as long as there is one goldfish no more than two inches long, no mosquito or gnat will live in the pond in its larval stage for long in its presence. It might also be thought that the water could become stagnant and smell, but no properly run pond will ever give off any bad smell. The original siting of the pond is very important as once it is made it may not be possible to change its position, if it is a concrete constructed one it would be impossible but a fibre glass or plastic one could be moved although not without a lot of trouble. When considering the position of the pond there are a few very important points to watch for. No pond should be sited under trees or too near bushes. As much sun as is possible should be able to reach the water as this encourages such plants as water lilies to flower at their best. At certain times of the year in the height of summer for instance it might be advisable to shade out some of the water, but this can easily be done with surface plants which will be described later. If the pond is badly sited it may not be possible to provide sufficient sunshine, but too much could always be cut down.

If the garden has any slope it is better to make the pond at the highest part. Any pond at a low level could be polluted by heavy rains washing unwanted matter into it. Also if the pond is on higher ground it is a fairly easy task to empty it if necessary even by siphon. Another point to consider is the availability of water for refilling or topping up at any time. Also if the pond can be constructed so that it is visible from the living-room of the house this will add to the pleasure, as even on wet days there may be fishes in the water which move around and make a living picture.

Should it be impossible to site the pond well away from

trees or shrubs it will be necessary to watch for falling leaves in the autumn as too many remaining in the water could cause pollution when they decay. Each morning or after strong winds the leaves could be netted from the surface

ROCKS ARRANGED IN A NATURAL DESIGN, NO STRAIGHT EDGES

before they sink down into the water. The presence of the leaves may not cause much trouble for a time but should the pond freeze over for any length of time, the foul gases caused by the decomposition of the leaves would be unable to escape and fresh oxygen could not enter the water. Such a condition could kill the fishes which would have been quite safe however cold the water became had it remained pure and well oxygenated.

If a rockery can be constructed at one side of the pond this will add to the beauty of the scene as it can provide a reflection of flowers and plants in the water giving double colour. When the soil is excavated for the pond it may be a problem where to deposit the soil, and what could be easier than to pile it up beside the pond and so form the basis of an attractive rockery? The amount of soil to be moved to make even a reasonably sized pond may come as a surprise to many people.

As well as making the rockery it is not difficult to arrange a water-fall to run down from a high level back into the pond. A small electric pump can be fitted so that a stream of water can flow into a small pool on the rockery. The water can then fall into another lower pool and over small falls flow back, so not only adding to the attraction of the pond but also to assist in reoxygenating the water.

If one is fortunate to have a small stream running through part of the garden it is possible to take the water from this so that the pond can be refilled at any time if necessary. If such a type of pond is constructed it must be made so that heavy flooding of the stream would not upset the balance of the pond. The best way would be to construct the pond near the running water and have a separate channel which can be shuttered off from the stream so that the flow of water can be controlled. It is not recommended to keep a flow of water continually running through the pond as some plants, especially water lilies do not like running water.

If it is not possible to construct a water-fall it may be quite simple to have a small fountain which can be switched on at any time necessary. Certain pumps are on the market which are submersible and can be lowered into the pond and be operated directly by electricity. Not only is a fountain an attraction to any garden but the effect on reoxygenating the water will have an advantage by keeping the fishes healthy, especially during hot weather.

The best time of the year to construct a pond is at the beginning of spring. It will then be possible to set up and stock it when water plants are starting to make fresh growth after the winter's rest. If a concrete pond is made late in the year it is better to wait until the spring before stocking it, but water can be left in to mature and assist in cleansing the concrete of any free lime which could cause harm to the fishes. It may not be possible to choose which time of the year to construct the pond but it should be remembered that if it is to be made with concrete it will be an advantage to make it when the weather is not too hot as concrete sets stronger if it does not do so too quickly.

# SETTING OUT THE POND

HAVING DECIDED where the pond is to be sited the next important consideration is as to its shape. This may be according to the shape of the garden or any flower bed arrangement. Where the garden has formal flower beds it will probably be better to keep to a formal shape for the pond as this will fit in better. The formal pond can be round, square or oblong, according to the shape of the garden but if the garden is informal in design then the pond will be better made irregularly.

If the garden is formal in design with oblong or square flower beds it may be possible to make the pond above ground by building up walls of concrete, bricks or broken paving stones. This raised pond can be made to look very attractive and one point in its favour is that little if any soil may have to be removed from the site. On the other hand such a pond is more liable to be damaged during severe frosts and could get warmer than a sunken pond during hot weather.

The next important point to be considered is the size of the pond. Due thought should be given to this and it may be of some help here to state that the smaller the pond the easier and cheaper it is to make but the more trouble and cost to maintain. Any very small pond will be subjected to many extremes of heat and cold and this could upset the fishes considerably. What is considered to be a small pond to many may not be the same for anyone with a large garden. Obviously the size must be related to the size of the garden as a very large pond in a small garden would be out of place and conversely. Try to arrange that the pond fits in with the general surroundings of the garden when it will look an attractive addition and not become too prominent.

Obviously it will not be possible to give any exact measurements for all requirements but I will suggest sizes which can be made and then individual conditions can be dealt with. A good sized garden pond, for growing water lilies as well as keeping and breeding fishes can be about twelve feet by eight, with a depth of two to two and a half feet. A small pond for a little garden could be half this size, but almost as deep, but any pond smaller than this cannot be considered to be a garden pond but not much more than a puddle. The sinking of a bath or old sink in the garden to be used as a pond is rather hopeless, as it will give a lot of trouble during extremes of weather and plants and fishes could not thrive in such a small area of water. Such containers can be used with advantage to breed certain types of live foods for the fishes, but there their usefulness ends.

Once the size and site have been decided it will be necessary to mark out the ground with great care. This is especially important when a formal shaped pond is to be constructed. A round pond must be exactly round and a square or oblong one very true at the corners. If this is not done the finished article will never look right. For a round pond drive a peg in the ground at the proposed centre. Then with string measure to the required half width. Tie a ring on one end and have a sharp stick at the other. With the ring over the centre stake it will be quite easy to mark out an exact circle. Pegs must now be driven in round this marking or a groove cut in the soil or grass.

For a formal shaped pond either square or oblong, it will be imperative to make sure that the corners are at right angles. If there is a straight path near the site it will be possible to insert two pegs parallel with it at the required length of the pond. Now place two pegs opposite to these at the desired width. Now measure the distance from opposite pegs, that is across from one end to the other at an angle. The distance between the two pegs from top to bottom at opposite corners should be exact and the pond will then have the correct right angles. If the pond is to be constructed of concrete, allow for the thickness of concrete when marking out. This will be stated when considering such construction.

If anyone wishes to breed or keep different species of fishes a very useful shape for the pond can be in the form of a cross. A centre part can be square and leading from it in the form of a cross can be four compartments, capable of being separated off individually. With such a pond it will be possible to divide off varying types of fishes or provide partitions where very small fishes would be safe from larger ones. It would also enable the pondkeeper to keep carnivorous fishes such as Perch or Pike away from those fishes which would be eaten in a mixed pond. When such a pond was being constructed it would be possible to arrange for some grooves to enable slides to be fitted when necessary. Whilst the concrete was still wet and soft, partitions of board or slate could be inserted after being wrapped in sheets of newspaper. When the concrete had set sufficiently the slides could be withdrawn. Another way would be to lightly paint the slides with oil before inserting, when they could be removed with ease. Discarded car engine oil is quite good for this purpose as long as sufficient is used to just cover the slides with none to run off.

To mark out an irregularly shaped pond the general position must be decided upon and then a clothes line or rope can be thrown down on the site. If first placed in a rough circle it can then be pushed out into any shape desired. By this means it is possible to create an informal shape which can then be marked out with pegs. The depth of the pond need never be more than two feet six. Any deeper pond would not necessarily be any better for plants or fishes. No water lily needs more than this depth in which to grow and fishes are quite safe during the winter if there is about this depth of water. The oxygen content of the water can vary considerably according to depth. Generally speaking the top third of the pond water will be well oxygenated and in a healthy condition for fishes. The middle third not quite so good and the bottom third much less so. Therefore very deep ponds are quite unnecessary either for plants or fishes.

It has often been recommended in the past that differing depths should be allowed for when making the pond so that water plants could be set in varying depths to suit their particular requirements. I consider that this is quite unnecessary and only making work for the constructor. If any plants need shallower depths it is quite easy to arrange this once the pond has been constructed by placing bricks or concrete blocks under the plant container. Not only does this enable the pond to be made more easily but it will be easier to clean out the pond at any future time.

# CONSTRUCTING THE POND

THE METHOD of construction of the pond depends on various factors. There are three main methods which can be used. They are concrete, plastic and fibre glass. The first method will mean more work but probably less cost although it could last longer than a plastic pond. Plastic ponds can be made with less trouble but for a fair sized one the cost can be rather high. The fibre glass ponds are usually on the small side and some of them are really too small to be considered as a garden pond. At the time of writing one about six feet by four and fifteen inches deep would cost about £14, and one eight feet by five with a depth of only a foot and a half could cost about £45.

A plastic pond about the size of the latter could cost about £6, for material. There are several types of plastic liners for ponds and as stout a type as possible should be used so that it could stand up to severe freezing of the water. A concrete pond could cost as much as a plastic lined one according to the local costs of aggregate and sand. The cement may not vary much in price in different localities but the proximity of a gravel or sand pit could have a decided effect on its price.

The concrete pond needs plenty of hard work to construct and it is a good idea to get the help of a friend when carrying out such a task as the mixing and applying of the

material is better done fairly quickly as some of the best cement for the purpose goes off, or starts to set, in a short space of time; with some types in half an hour. It is often suggested that shuttering has to be used when constructing a concrete pond. To use this would put up the cost at least by three times as timber is very expensive and metal shuttering would be costly to hire. I consider that it is quite unnecessary to use any form of shuttering. No pond needs to be made with perpendicular sides, no matter whether it is to be of a formal shape or irregular. Natural ponds have a side which has a gradual slope and rarely at an angle exceeding 45°. If the pond is made with sloping sides it will be possible to float the concrete into position without using any form of shuttering.

The easiest method for constructing the pond is undoubtedly the using of a fibre glass one. All that is then necessary is to decide on the site, buy the fibre shape and dig out the soil to the required shape. The fibre pond can then be put in position and filled with water immediately. It could even be made and stocked in one day although I do not recommend placing fishes into any pond until the water plants have had a chance to get established. Still it could be done and so for anyone who is rather impatient to see the finished product the fibre glass pool is the answer. I do have reservations about this type at present as it does appear that those available today are hardly large enough for the purpose of keeping and breeding a number of fishes.

A plastic lined pond can be made much larger than a fibre glass one but there are one or two points which must be watched when using this material. In the first place there are several makes on the market, the best type is a stout form with reinforcement in the form of artificial netting insertion. A fairly heavy type should be used as this will stand a better chance of remaining undamaged during a severe frost. Also this reinforced material could be obtained at almost any size to suit the requirements for any garden. Sizes are available up to twenty feet by ten and it is also possible to get larger sheets specially made when the material is welded together. The cost of the last mentioned size would be about £27, at the time of writing.

If a pond is to be made with the heavy sheeting it must be remembered when ordering that the sheet will be stretched down into position in the pond when filled with water and so allowance must be made for this so that there is sufficient overlap to reach the sides of the pond. Some plastic liners are of varying colours and can be bought to suit individual tastes. It is possible to purchase some with a stone-like finish and even to resemble pebbles. Once the sheet is obtained and the position marked out, the soil can be removed. Sightings must be made as the excavation goes on to ensure that the top of the finished pond will be quite level. A spirit level on a long board should be used to ensure that a level top is obtained. If not, when filled with water, the whole appearance could be spoilt by having three or four inches of space at one side of the pond and water over-flowing at the other.

Having removed all the soil, a very close inspection should be made to make sure that there are no sharp stones left in the bottom or sides of the excavation. Such sharp material could perhaps puncture the lining when pressure from water was exerted. Where stones are a problem it may be better to line the pond with fine sand before adding the lining. In any case the excavation should be well hammered down with the back of a spade or similar object to make certain that a good firm base is provided for the plastic sheeting.

If the sheeting is of a good type it can then be laid in the hole. Some should stretch over the sides and this can be lightly secured with slabs of stone. If the liner is of the special stretching type it is possible to lay it over the hole, secure it at the sides with slabs and then run in the water. The liner will then conform to the shape of the hole by stretching as the weight of water presses it down. Once the pond is filled the liner which extends around the top of the pond can be trimmed off if too wide and paving slabs can be laid all around the edge to make a path and to keep the edges of the liner secure and hidden. If the slabs protrude over the edge of the pond a little, this will enhance the appearance of the pond. Any wrinkles in the material will soon disappear once the weight of water takes effect.

Once this type of pond has been filled it is possible to start stocking it right away. It is probable that there will be no ill effects from the plastic but if it is well washed before being used this would remove any powder or dust which may have covered it. The stocking of the ponds will be dealt with in a later chapter.

To construct a concrete pond it will be necessary to get together sufficient quantities of material before a start is made. Once concreting has commenced it is most important to try to finish all this work at one go as if part of the work is left for some hours it is possible that a good join will not be made to this with the fresh concrete. Such a join may be a weak spot in the pond at a future date. The thickness of concrete to make a good job must be not less than three inches for fairly small ponds and four or five inches for larger ones. Some reinforcing material can be included especially for a large pond or for any which has any angles. Even a few reinforcing bars at the corners will perhaps be sufficient. Some stout galvanised wire can be used as the cement will adhere very strongly to this.

The cement you use must be fresh, not full of lumpy pieces which indicate staleness or that it has been in a damp atmosphere. Some aggregate must be obtained. This is a rather coarse form of gravel with stones up to an inch across together with smaller ones. Also some very sharp, coarse sand must be purchased. The type of sand known as washed sand or grit will do. Soft sand is useless especially if such sand includes lumps of clay-like matter. This could cause a leak if used. Cement can be obtained which is quick drying and also some which is waterproof. Also it is possible to tint it with colouring agents but this is not essential as any pond will soon become more natural looking as Algæ grows on it.

For a medium sized pond it is probable that about a cubic yard of concrete will be necessary but the depth of the pond and the thickness of concrete to be used will all have to be allowed for. To make such a quantity of concrete the following amounts of material will be needed :— Three quarters of a yard of aggregate, half a yard of sand and six cwt., of cement. The sand and aggregate should be well mixed and then the cement added. The whole should be turned over three times before any water is added. The water should be added gradually from a rose watering can. Another three turns of the mixture should be given before it is ready. Do not make the mixture too wet, if it appears on the dry side it is probable that it will look better as it is worked into position. If too wet it can slip down the side of the pond whereas a good texture will stay in position.

There are two ways of using the concrete. One is to mix a rather stoney one with little sand at first with some cement and place this in position. Then make up a mixture of one part cement to three parts sand and apply this on the first coat as soon as the first has set sufficiently to remain firm. This top coat can be floated on about an inch thick. The surface need not be worked to a smooth finish as the more it is worked the more likely it is to slide down. When the first method is used it is possible by gently tamping the mixture to bring up the fine matter to the surface a really good strong job can be obtained but by the latter method it is possible that the second coat may not adhere firmly at all points and so may arise the possibility of a leak after some time.

The speed with which the concrete can be placed in position will decide whether the pond is likely to remain strong and waterproof for ever afterwards. If a concrete path is required around the pond do not under any circumstances make this path continuous with the concrete in the pond. If this is done it is almost certain that with the first very heavy frost the ground under the path will expand as the earth freezes. This will push up the path and a crack will occur round the top of the pond, perhaps just below water level when leaks will occur. Any path made should be quite separate from the pond and is better made with concrete slabs or broken paving stones. Another thing to bear in mind is that if two adjoining ponds are made be careful to ensure that the concrete has set before filling with water. If you do not do this it is possible that the join between the two ponds will break under the weight of the water on either side.

Once the concrete has been laid in position it is important to make sure that it does not dry out too quickly. If this happens the finished pond may not be as strong as if the concrete had been allowed to set more slowly. It is therefore better to make the pond during cooler weather if possible. If it does turn hot whilst the concrete is setting it should be sprayed with water, not too strongly but enough to damp it all over. A good cement should enable the mixture to set in two or three days but do not be in a hurry to fill it with water until you are sure that it has set sufficiently to be able to withstand the weight of water required to fill it. Although it is not advised to make such a pond during hot weather neither should it be done during frosty weather. A severe frost on the concrete before it has set will cause damage to the surface and peeling could occur.

If any reinforcing wires are used they must be pushed into position as the concrete is being laid so that they are about the centre of the layer of concrete. It is possible to construct a bottom outlet for the pond if this is desired. In such a case it is necessary to dig down well below the base of where the pond will rest and incorporate a quantity of broken bricks as a drainage hole. When the pond is being made the outlet can be inserted. This could be a stone bottle with a strong stopper. The end of the bottle is cut off and the stopper allowed to project into the pond where it could be reached if it was intended to empty the pond. The objection to this is that the outlet could become blocked with mud or detritus and small fishes could escape from the pond.

Providing the concrete pond has been constructed properly it is possible for it to remain waterproof for very many years. Causes of failure can be due to improper mixing, stale cement, spongey matter in the sand, too long intervals between the application of a second coat to the first and too fast a drying out.

If it is intended to construct a type of water-fall with the pond it may be necessary to arrange for its entry at the time of construction of the pond. The part of the pond where the water will enter must be made in one with the pond or if left until a later date it may not be possible to get a good join. However it would always be possible to make a water-fall at any later time by making sure that the lip of the fall over-hung the top of the pond. A very attractive fall can be made with the aid of one or two plastic or fibre pools. These fibre glass pools can be obtained ready made with lips provided to allow the water to run from one small pool to another and so eventually into the pond. If these pools are made with concrete it will be necessary to take care that water cannot leak through the joints from one pool to another. The water-fall will have to be worked by an electric pump which can be housed in a water-proof box near the pond. The inlet pipe must have a strainer attached to prevent it becoming blocked by detritus. Another pipe can carry the water up to the top of the water-fall. All pipes and joins in pools can be carefully hidden by the use of rock work, and although the result may not look quite natural when first made it is probable that after a short space of time when the plants have grown and the stone-work matured the whole appearance will be changed for the better. When installing the system or even when introducing an underwater working fountain avoid using any metal such as copper or brass. Certain fishes can be killed by a fifth part of copper to a million parts of water. A little copper may not be as dangerous at one time but if water continually flows through copper pipes the result can be the loss of many fishes.

The type of fountain which can be purchased can be placed directly into the pond with no other trouble than seeing that the connecting electric cable is hidden from view. This can be done by covering it with a slab or run-

A WATERFALL ADDS
INTEREST TO A GARDEN.

ning underneath one which surrounds the pond. These
cables are supplied capable of being used in water. Any
switch needed for operating either the fall or fountain
should be out of sight if possible but capable of being
switched on by a grown up and not low enough for a
child.

A type of pond which is very popular in a formal garden
is a raised one. This enables one to watch the fishes in the
water much better as they can be nearer to eye level. To
make such a pond requires rather more skill than it does to
make a sunken pond  The outside structure has to be very
well made to enable it to withstand the vagaries of the
weather. A depth of at least two feet is necessary but this
does not mean that the pond will have to have walls two
feet high. Part of the pond can be sunken so that only a
foot or a foot and a half stands up above the ground level.
The required depth can then be taken out of the ground. A
formal shaped pond will have to be made, either round
which will be more difficult to construct or square or oblong
in shape.

The choice of material for building up the sides is
important as any soft bricks would soon become useless
after a few severe winters. Either use a hard brick or stone
work such as broken paving stones. A good foundation will
have to be made first all round the pond. This should be
at least a foot deep, constructed with concrete. Once this
has set well the building can be started. When placing any
building material where water will eventually reach do not
fill in with mortar the joins between bricks or slabs. When
the walls are of sufficient height and the mortar has set,
the inside can receive attention. If the pond is to be deeper
than the level of the brickwork, the soil must be removed
and the ground well firmed as for making an ordinary

concrete pond. The cavity can now be concreted as for the pond and as the brickwork ·is reached the compost can be forced into the crevices left on the inside of the brickwork. The concrete should come up a little above the desired height of water in the pond to avoid any chance of a leak at this junction.

The effect of broken paving stones for the wall will be much better than that obtained by using bricks. Any wall should be not less than a foot wide and a little more if it is intended to have water well up the sides of the wall. When water is required almost up to the top of the wall the concrete on the inside must be continued up to the desired height without any break or a leak will occur at this point. It is essential that a good strong job should be made when constructing the walls as if the frost caused great expansion of the ice in the pond the outer structure could be damaged. The top of the wall could be finished off with a row of concrete slabs and an attractive garden pond would be the result. The force exerted by freezing water must never be lost sight of when constructing any pond. It has been said that if a pond is made with sloping sides the ice will never crack it as the ice will slide up the sides of the pond as it forms. A happy idea but it is utter nonsense. Once even half an inch of ice forms on the side of a concrete pond nothing could ever move it a fraction of an inch until it is thawed. The advantage of making a pond with sloping sides is that shuttering can be dispensed with and the pond will be more natural for the fishes and the water will probably keep in a better condition because the light has a better chance of reaching the water at the bottom.

If a garden has a good slope from one end to the other it is possible to make a very attractive water scene by having one fairly large pond at the higher point. A small stream can then be continued from it into other smaller pools and eventually through another channel to a small pond in which is included a small electric pump. This pump will send the water back to the highest pond. An electric pump of about half horse power would be sufficient and even one half that power would be enough to work such a series of pools and streams if not too long.

When constructing the various pools and channels it is important to make sure that any joins are leakproof. This can be ensured by seeing that the upper lip protrudes out over the lower pool to prevent any loss of water. When constructing any form of pond with a water-fall one must bear in mind that once the pump is started to work from the lower pool, the water level in it will fall considerably and so allowance must be made by seeing that this feeder pool is deep enough and large enough to make certain that it is not almost emptied when the pump is switched on.

The possibility of using a small running stream in the garden as a feeder for a garden pond has been mentioned. Where such a system is possible it is necessary to so construct the inlet from the stream so that it can be controlled. It may also be possible, if the fall of the land allows it, to make an outlet from the pond so that if at any time fresh water needed to run into it, shutters or slides could be operated allowing the stream water to pass through it. I do not recommend having water continually running through a garden pond as if water lilies are growing in the pond they may not thrive. These plants are not usually happy in running water. The slight flow of water from a small water-fall would not be enough to upset the lilies as this would not probably be strong enough to disturb the general composition of water.

An interesting type of pond could be made by any

handyman which has an observation window incorporated in it. Such a pond would have to be so planned that it would be possible to construct an outside well or pit where one could stand to view the underwater inhabitants of the pond. This observation chamber could be constructed after the pond had been completed. A sheet of plate glass must be obtained which is fitted into the side of the pond as the concrete is placed in position. Make sure that it is at the desired height and that it is well embedded into the concrete. Another method of inserting the glass would be to force a piece of metal sheet or stout timber into the concrete as it is laid. The sheet should be about an inch larger than the glass which it is intended to use. If this sheet is oiled it can be removed when the concrete is set and then the glass can be fitted with good aquarium putty. If the glass was set in during construction the outside could be cleaned quite easily of any cement still adhering.

Once the pond was made the outside chamber could be excavated with a few steps to allow one to go down below to watch the fishes through the glass. When such a chamber is made it is important to make sure that a drainage sump has been provided at the bottom or it might become flooded after heavy rains.

Some gardeners like to have a bog garden incorporated with the pond and this is a good idea where conditions allow. The bog garden should be continuous with the pond so that bog plants can meet and blend with the water plants. One of the best ways of constructing the bog garden is to use heavy plastic sheeting continuous with the pond. The ground should be excavated to a foot or two from where the sheeting will lie. This can then be filled with peaty soil which will provide a suitable spot for many of the bog and water-side plants to flourish.

Another method of creating a bog garden is to so construct one side of the pond that a small over-flow allows surplus water to run over to a particular spot where the bog garden is required. In times of drought when it might be possible for the bog garden to get too dry it would be possible to run some water into the pond so that it could over-flow and so keep the bog garden wet. If such an over-flow is constructed it is advisable to incorporate a small screen, perforated zinc would do, to prevent any small fishes from being washed over the top. Suitable plants for this garden will be described in a later chapter.

Whilst describing the different methods of constructing a garden pond no mention has been made for providing shelves or pockets in which plants can be set. The making of these shelves can be difficult when dealing with plastic liners. However there is no need to make any such shelves as if any plants require a shallower water position this can be easily done by raising the plant container on bricks or slabs. One good type of pond has one deeper part, up to two and a half feet, and this can be where the water lily is planted. The rest of the pond need not be more than eighteen inches deep. As long as one part of the pond is fairly deep there is no need to keep the whole base at the same level. The deep part not only gives depth for the lily but fishes can swim down into it during very cold weather.

If the pond contains no shelves nor pockets it will make the task of cleaning out the pond far easier. The use of a quantity of soil in the bottom of the pond or even a lot of sand is quite unnecessary. All water plants can be set in a separate container. This makes planting easier and when the pond has to be cleaned out the containers can be removed easily. This method also ensures that it is possible to control the growth of the plants in the following years.

# A RECTANGULAR POOL

WATER LEVEL

2'6" Deep end
1'6" Shallow end

18"

6"

Shuttering securely battened & braced

1" boarding

Line of excavation

6" wide trench for concrete, remove blocks as concrete is placed.

Ground level

## SHUTTERING IN PLACE FOR CONCRETING

If such plants are set in a base of compost their roots would become entangled in a short space of time that it would be very difficult to move any plant or to control it. Most water plants become very rampant after a year or two and once the base compost became riddled with roots it would be a major task to keep control of them.

There has been almost a revolution in methods of constructing garden ponds during the past few years. Formally it was only possible by using concrete, a tough job for anyone but the very active. Today there are so many types of liners that pond construction has been made quite simple. The most important point to watch when purchasing the liner is to make sure that it is of sufficient strength to withstand some years of wear. The ordinary plastic sheeting is not strong enough for a sound job but any liner with reinforcement or of the very strong pliable type will be quite safe to use. All the necessary requirements for a perfect pond can now be obtained, as dealers specialise in providing all the materials and accessories necessary for constructing ponds, water-falls and fountains. Electric pumps can also be bought which can work falls, fountains and also be used for emptying the pond if necessary. A look through the advertisement columns of most gardening magazines will usually provide information and addresses of the specialist dealers for all needs of the pond-keeper.

To sum up the construction of ponds it will be useful to give the important features to watch for. They are:— Correct siting, as the pond cannot be moved afterwards, especially if it is made with concrete; do make the pond large enough to function properly and provide a suitable place for water plants and where fishes can thrive and probably breed. Although a larger pond may cost more in the first place it will save money afterwards in obviating the cost of replacing dying plants and fishes.

When considering making a pond it is well to consider providing plenty of swimming space for fishes as a pond without healthy fishes is like a bird cage without a bird. Also the fishes will ensure that any harmful insects which could breed in the pond will stand no chance of surviving in their presence.

# FILLING AND MATURING THE POND

THE TIME for filling the pond will depend largely on how it was constructed. The fibre glass and plastic lined ponds can be filled immediately and if the stretch type sheeting was used then the water will have been supplied as the sheeting was pressed to the shape of the pond. A concrete pond will require a different treatment as cement can give off harmful lime in the water for some time. This free lime can kill fishes and so it is most important to make sure that this is removed before any fishes are placed in the pond. Some types of quick setting waterproof cements do not give off as much free lime as ordinary cement. There are solutions on the market which can be painted over the concrete to prevent this lime from entering the water. Although this method can be used it is possible to make the water quite safe by ordinary washings.

Once the concrete has set the pond should be filled with water. It is then left for a couple of days and then partially emptied. The sides of the pond can then be well scrubbed with a stiff broom. Wash round after emptying all the old water, refill and repeat the treatment after two or three more days. This will remove any free lime and the next filling can remain to be planted when possible. Where concrete ponds are concerned it must be remembered that

36

the deeper the pond the less will be the concentration of free lime in the water when first filled. A shallow pond will have so much more concrete in contact with the small amount of water that the concentration of lime will be greater.

If any form of paint is used on the concrete make sure that it is a good type as poor ones could flake away and so expose fresh concrete which might give off lime. If the inside of the pond was painted with any colour with the object of improving the look of the fresh concrete, there is always the danger that this might become loosened by the action of the water and so spoil the whole look of the pond. There is no need to use any top colouring as it is possible to buy colouring agents for mixing with the cement when it is used. I consider this quite unnecessary as in a short time the sides of the pond will become covered with minute forms of vegetation and the sides of the pond will take on a natural look, and any colouring matter used will soon be hidden.

Once the pond is filled do not be in a hurry to stock it. The water will mature when in contact with the air. Tap water can be used, as after a few days it will have lost any effect of chlorination which may have been present when first drawn from the tap. As copper dissolved in water can be very dangerous to fishes it is rather a problem for the pondkeeper whose water system includes copper pipes. Such systems are far more common nowadays and the best method to adopt when filling a pond from copper pipes is to allow some water to run to waste before allowing any to run into the pond. New copper pipes can be more dangerous than older ones and in districts where the water is soft the danger may be increased. Where the water contains lime it is probable that the pipes will have been encrusted with a coating of lime and the danger from copper poisoning will be lessened.

Many people imagine that it is better to use rain water than tap, but this depends a great deal on how the rain water is caught. If from any roof, especially near a town, such water will be far from pure. If rain water could be obtained from a perfectly clean roof it could be quite safe but most rain water coming from a house roof would be so contaminated by soot and filth that it would be quite dangerous to use it for the pond if it contained any fishes. The truth of this can be tested by tying an old sock over the end of the down pipe from the roof. After a few days this will contain a large quantity of soot and other undesirable matter which would do no good to the pond. If rain water could be caught after heavy rains have well washed the roof the water could be safer.

Although tap water can be used for fishes it is well to try to get rid of as much chlorine as possible. If tap water stands in the open for some hours it usually becomes quite safe. When introducing fresh tap water into a pond at any time it is a good plan to either use a rose spray at the end or play the water on the side of the pond so that it is well broken up making it much purer. When adding fresh tap water to an established pond any ill effects from chlorination would soon be nulified when it is mixed with the matured pond water. The presence of growing water plants in the pond would also tend to eliminate any harmful effects from the tap water.

It is probable that it will take ten days to a fortnight to get a concrete pond safe for fishes, but other types of construction used could mean that plants could be introduced after a couple of days. Although water plants could be added it would not be wise to introduce any fishes for a time. Once the plants are growing and look established the fishes can be added. I do not recommend doing this for at least a fortnight after the plants have been in the pond. The action of the growing plants can assist in purifying the water and so help to make it safe for the fishes.

If any water-falls have been incorporated in the scheme it is necessary to run plenty of water through them to remove any harmful matter before filling the pond for the last time. If any of the fibre glass pools have been used in the construction there should be nothing harmful to come from them. Where concrete channels or falls have been made with no fibre glass pools it is very important to thoroughly wash them to remove any free lime. The pump should be kept running for several hours for a day or two to well wash the concrete.

# PLANTING THE POND

NO POND will function properly unless it has growing water plants. Neither can it ever look as attractive as one which has a suitable collection of plants which can provide plenty of flowers and so increase the attractiveness of the pond all through the warmer months of the year. Once the pond water has matured the next consideration is when to plant. All the usual water plants start to grow in the spring and so this is the best time to introduce them. From April right throughout the summer plants can be set and they will soon grow and assist in keeping the water in good condition. If any water plants had been grown in containers they could be added to the pond earlier than suggested but they would just remain dormant until the water warmed up a little.

Apart from the beautifying effect of flowers in the pond water plants can serve a very useful purpose. There are three main types of water plants which can be used. They are under-water oxygenating ones, those with their roots well down in the pond and floating ones. The oxygenating plants are very important as not only do they assist in using up foul gases but they give off oxygen in the water for the benefit of the inhabitants. Most of them also use up much of the waste matter in the pond by their roots. These roots can become very numerous and spreading over the bottom of the pond. They appear to have the power to attract floating mulm and detritus to them so that their cleansing action of the water can effect large areas. The droppings from the fishes will soon disintegrate in the water and this matter is adequately dealt with by the roots of the submerged water plants. The underwater plants are then a must for any garden pond.

The second type of water plant includes the water lilies. They are the finest plants for any pond as their spectacular flowers cannot fail to give pleasure right through the summer from late May to October. No pond should be without a water lily and no pond should be made so small that it cannot house at least one such plant. Apart from providing a show of beautiful flowers there is another useful feature which makes them a must and that is when they are growing well they send out many roots, often well outside their containers. These roots also attract much of the waste matter in the pond and utilise it, thus helping to keep the water pure. Many of the other water plants act in the same way having their roots working hard at the bottom of the pond and sending up their leaves and flowers above the water.

There is also a third benefit to be obtained from this type of water plant. Some of them spread their leaves over the surface of the water and so shade out much of the sun during the warmer times of the year. This has the effect of restricting the growth of green Algae which could otherwise thrive in the sunny water and make the pond water a thick green condition. The water lily leaves are about the best for this purpose and when shading out the strong light they also provide a shady place for the fishes to rest in. These plants do not give off oxygen in the water like the submerged ones and their use is therefore confined to the provision of flowers, assisting to use up waste matter and by giving a certain amount of shade.

There is a very important consideration when setting any of those plants which use up waste matter and that is the method of planting. It has often been recommended to plant water liles with a good rich compost, even some containing cow manure is also advised. I do not go along with this view as I consider that when the needs of fishes are also considered in the pond it is far better to use a poorer type of compost. This will encourage the water lily to send out more roots to search for nourishment which it will find among the droppings from the fishes and other waste matter. The better you feed your lilies at the outset the less will they be inclined to work for you in the pond. The farmer who keeps cats to kill rats and mice in his barns does not over-feed the cats or they would become lazy, and water plants act in the same way.

The third type of water plant is the floating kind. These may send down small roots into the water but they are free floating and do not become anchored. They can be used for shutting out much of the light from the water and this is the reason why some experienced pondkeepers grow a quantity of duck weed so that it shades the pond and assists in keeping the green Algae under control. There are other floating plants which flower and whilst they also serve a useful purpose, too many floating plants could cover too much of the water and so the inhabitants could be hidden from view.

There are so many fine species and varieties of water lily that it is difficult to recommend any one by name as people may have particular fancies for certain colours. The best way to choose is to study a catalogue and make your choice. If one is not sure which to have then the best method is to ask the supplier to let you have the ones most suited for your purpose. All that would be necessary would be to give the size and depth of the pond and the colour of flower you would prefer. You would then get kinds which would flourish under your conditions.

Lilies are best planted in special crates supplied by dealers as these crates are of a plastic material which will not rot in water. They are also openwork in construction which will allow the roots to spread out into the surrounding water. Large clay pots can be used if they have plenty of drainage holes near the base. When using one it is wise to set the pot into a small heap of freshly mixed concrete with paper underneath. When the concrete has set the paper can be peeled off and a firm base to the pot will prevent it from falling over when in the water.

I suggest that all the compost that is necessary for a lily is some old turf. This is packed round the outside of the crate and the root-stock of the lily firmly fixed inside. As before stated I do not recommend using any fertilisers if fish keeping is desired in the pond; if the pond is intended as a lily pond only then added fertilisers can increase the growth of the lily. I have always found that the trouble never arises when a water lily does not grow adequately; the reverse is the case as in a year or two some can become so rampant that they take over the whole pond. Another happening when the lily grows well is that the ample leaf structure floating on the surface can exert such a pull that the whole plant floats to the surface. To obviate this from happening a couple of lengths of plastic cord can be tied over the crown of the lily in its container to prevent any subsequent movement.

The number of lilies to a pond is very important. Many pondkeepers start with too many plants and after a year or two find that their pond has lost much of its beauty. If water lilies become too crowded much of their attraction is of no more value than if they had been ordinary plants growing in the garden. The ideal pond is one with not much more than a third of its surface covered with water lily leaves. The water should always be very obvious so that fishes within can be seen and that they are able to reach the top of the water if necessary. Once a lily grows too big for the pond the leaves cannot find a space on top of the water. Instead many will grow up into the air, looking anything but attractive, no water will be visible and one might just as well have no pond at all.

The larger growing lilies are of no use in a small shallow pond but small growing types could be accommodated in large ponds providing they are grown away from stronger ones and have their container raised to the required depth by bricks or slabs. This raising of the container is also important when planting almost any lily as they appear to grow better if they are not placed too deeply at first. As leaves are formed the lily could be lowered by the removal of all or some of the bricks.

I will give a few names of suitable lilies for the varying depths of ponds but it is not intended here to make this book a catalogue of water plants as their numbers are legion. Rather I advise the pondkeeper to seek advice from the expert dealer. However the following may help to give ideas. For a shallow pond with a depth of twelve to eighteen inches of water; try, *Nymphaea laydeckeri purpurata,* with flowers of a rather deep rose crimson; *N. odorata alba,* which is a good scented white; *N. rose nymph,* is one of the finest pinks. Two more which can grow in as little as nine inches are *N. pygmaea helvola* and *N. pygmaea alba*; the first a yellow and the other white. If there was a shallow shelf in the pond these two could be grown there but to make a pond with so little depth, especially for these would be asking for trouble.

Some excellent lilies for the pond about $1\frac{1}{2}$ to 2 feet deep are:—*N. escarboucle,* crimson and free flowering; *N. James Brydon,* another deep rose coloured flower and a good grower; *N. marliacea rosea,* pale pink and handsome; *N. aurea,* a buff-yellow; *N. candida,* white and a fine type; *N. Marliacea albida,* another good white; and *N. virginale,* also a fine white. For a deep pond choose from:— *N. Chas de Meurville,* a deep pink; *N. gladstonia,* and *N. colossea,* a pale pink.

Although lilies have been recommended for the varying depths it is possible to grow most of them in rather a more varied depth. Some of them will grow less and produce smaller flowers when planted in restricted space, and some of the smaller lilies can grow larger with good treatment. When planting remember to allow for a fair depth of soil in the container or your rootstock may be too near the surface when placed in the water.

There are a number of other water plants which are similar in use for breaking up the flatness of the pond. These are not oxygenating plants but use up much of the waste matter in the pond, can provide some shade in summer and give some flowers. The following can be chosen:—*Acorus calamus variegatus,* a pretty rush; *Butomus umbellatus,* a fine flowering rush with pink heads of flowers; *Caltha palustris plena,* a double yellow flower; *Iris kaempferi,* can be used as a water plant or as a bog plant; there are many varieties of this and one can choose which colour is required; *Sagittaria japonica flor pleno,* this is a splendid plant as it sends up heart-shaped leaves and then flowers with a rich double white flower like a miniature carnation. *Pontederia cordata,* is also excellent. There are many plants suitable for the pond side or bog garden. Many which will grow in shallow water can also be grown in the bog garden where the soil never gets dry. Some of the finest for such places are the Primulas and the Mimulus. It would be difficult to go far wrong with any of the hardy primulus as they delight in damp conditions. Types of primulas such as *P. bulleyana*; *P. denticulata* and *P. sikkimensis,* are excellent and can be had in several colours. Some of the newer mimulus are very attractive with larger and more colourful flowers than the old fashioned types. Another fine range of water side plants can be found among the Astilbes. These have handsome divided foliage and flower with feather-like sprays in various colours. The Trolius varieties are also very useful. There are so many suitable plants for the shallow water or pond side that could be used but it must be borne in mind that most of them will become very rampant when established and so pruning or dividing may become necessary after the first year.

The very important oxygenating plants will be described next. These plants grow completely under water and assist in keeping the water pure. When planting any of these it must be realised that they will soon grow and can take over much of the pond. It is therefore a waste of money to plant too many of them. Also some may not be seen very much although they may be doing a good job in the water. Some can be introduced into the water in small bunches with a strip of lead to anchor them. These soon become established. Others can be rooted first in a small plastic container, covered with water in another container. When these grow they can be placed in the pond with the small pot. As most of the plants recommended will soon

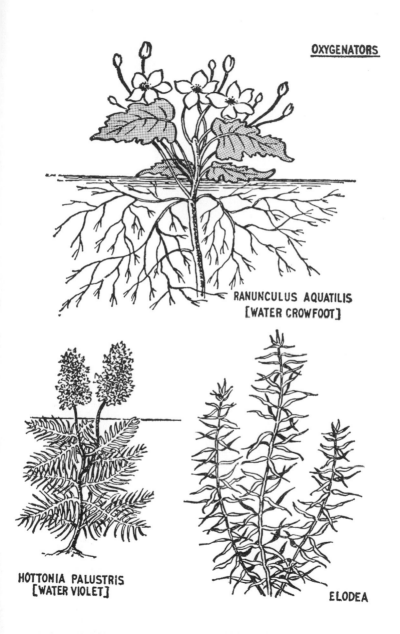

RANUNCULUS AQUATILIS
[WATER CROWFOOT]

HOTTONIA PALUSTRIS
[WATER VIOLET]

ELODEA

spread in the pond there is no need to plant several kinds. Some may become more rampant than others and choke them out. In any small pond just one type of oxygenating plant can be used. No more than three kinds need be placed in any pond.

One of the very best for the pond without any base soil or gravel is *Ceratophyllum demersum*, or Hornwort. This plant never makes roots but establishes itself in the mulm at the bottom. It also appears to have the power to attract waste matter to it. The long stems are covered with fine leaves in whorls and not only is it a good oxygenator but it makes a grand receptacle for the eggs of fishes.

Another excellent plant is *Lagarosiphon major*, which was formerly known as *Elodea crispa*. This plant throws out long stems which are covered with narrow leaves which curl back over the stems, it is one of the best oxygenators. Another good one is *Egeria densa*, previously known as *Elodea densa*. This is rather similar to the previous plant described but the leaves do not curl back as much. These three plants mentioned are all that are necessary in any pond. There are several other suitable ones but none will give better service than those named. Such species as *Elodea canadensis*, although a good oxygenator can become very rampant, tangle up with other plants and often gets covered with blanket weed. Other kinds are:—Starwort; Willow Moss; Water Crowfoot and Curled Pond-weed, (*Potamogeton*). These can be used if the first three described are unavailable. Water Crowfoot, *Ranunculus aquatilis*, can be grown in a large pond as it can look very attractive in the spring. The under water leaves are very thin but small, almost round shiny ones are grown on the surface and then pretty white flowers are produced, like white buttercups.

Floating aquatics are the plants which remain mostly on the surface of the water and do not send their roots down into the mulm or mud at the bottom. These are not oxygenating plants but provide some shade from too much sunshine. They serve a very useful purpose in the summer to assist in keeping down the growth of green Algae which soon turns the water a thick green so that the fishes cannot be seen. One of the most useful for the purpose is *Lemna minor*, or Duck weed. This plant has small thick shiny leaves which float on the surface and small roots hang down in the water. A good covering of this plant will often clear a pond of green Algae. Some pondkeepers complain that once it is introduced it is difficult to clear from the pond. Although it can grow and spread fairly rapidly, it can be easily removed from the pond by playing a strong hose on it from one side. The Duck weed can then be rolled over to one side when it can be raked out. A medium sized pond can be cleared of the weed in ten minutes. Some may grow again but if there are some hungry goldfish in the pond they will eat much of the weed.

Duck weed seeds drop to the bottom of the pond in late autumn and grow again in the spring. A species of this weed is *Lemna major*, which is also useful but not quite as common. Another species, *Lemna trisulca*, commonly known as the Ivy-leaved Duck weed, grows partly submerged except in the summer but this one is not recommended as it soon becomes a thick mass and is liable to get coated with blanket weed. The Water Hyacinth, *Eichornia speciosa*, is a handsome floating plant which makes rosettes on the surface and sends up pale violet flowers. This plant is not hardy in some parts of the country and so can be potted up for the winter and kept in a place safe from frost. It need only be kept damp, and soon grows when placed in the pond in the spring. The Water Soldier, *Stratiotes aloides*, also makes rosettes of serrated leaves and has a white flower. After flowering the plant sinks to the bottom. It is not of much use in the pond but can look attractive when in flower.

It must be realised that these floating aquatics are not necessary if there is a good covering of water lily leaves on the surface but before these have made good growth the floaters are useful for cutting out much of the strong sunlight, and some such as the Duck weed form a very useful food for omnivorous fishes. Most of the under-water oxygenating plants die down in the late autumn and reappear in the spring. Until they do so the pond may become rather green through an excess of floating green Algae. This is a plant and can give off oxygen but if it gets too thick in the water it can become unsightly and the fishes will not be seen. At such times a few floating acquatics can be very useful for shading out much of the light. Once the water lily leaves cover some of the surface the floating plants could be dispensed with.

Many pondkeepers new to the hobby are inclined to over-stock with plants and after a year or so the pond can become choked with them and the fishes cannot find sufficient swimming space. Try to look ahead and only plant enough plants to function without drastic pruning for at least three years. By planting most of the water plants in separate containers it is possible to control their growth but if soil and gravel has been placed on the bottom in the first instance and the plants have become strongly established in this it is very difficult to keep them under control in after years.

# STOCKING THE POND

ONCE THE water plants have become established and started to grow the stocking of the pond will be the next consideration. Many pondkeepers are impatient to get some fish in the pond but it is far better to wait until the water has matured well and the plants are making enough growth to function properly. When signs of active growth are apparent and the water appears to be in good condition it will be time to introduce the fishes.

As with the water plants so it is with the inhabitants, do not over-stock in the first place as if all goes well the fishes will grow and probably breed. One must not be misguided by the numbers of fishes often seen in the tanks of dealers. Try to imagine how many specimens are likely to be in a similar amount of water in a lake, river or pond in natural conditions. If a section of water the size of your pond could be taken from a lake and examined it is doubtful if it would contain many fishes of all types and so one must not try to house more fishes in the pond than will remain in good health and thrive. The necessary number of fishes for a particular pond cannot be stated conclusively as depth as well as size can have an influence. When dealing with an indoor tank it is usual to allow 24 square inches of surface area to each inch of fish not counting the tail, but with a pond this could be too much as fishes are

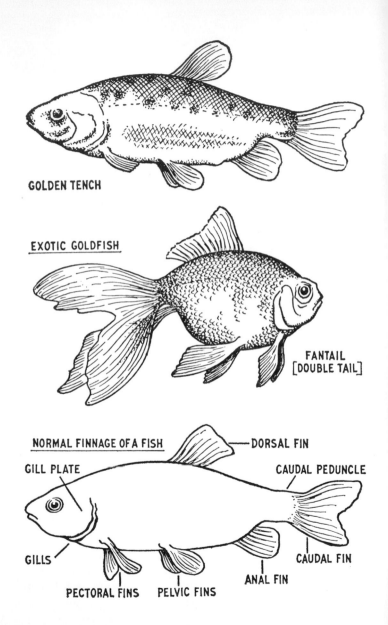

GOLDEN TENCH

EXOTIC GOLDFISH

FANTAIL
[DOUBLE TAIL]

NORMAL FINNAGE OF A FISH

DORSAL FIN

GILL PLATE

CAUDAL PEDUNCLE

GILLS

CAUDAL FIN

PECTORAL FINS

PELVIC FINS

ANAL FIN

more likely to make rapid growth in a pond than they would do in a tank.

For a pond 6 feet by 4 feet and 18 inches deep, 10 small fishes would be enough. For a pond 10 by 6 feet and about 2 feet deep, 18 small fishes would be sufficient. Some kinds of fishes grow much quicker than others and these will be described when naming suitable kinds. It is not a good policy to buy large fishes in the first place. They may look very nice when introduced but they may not thrive as well as smaller ones. The small ones would not have known different conditions for such a long time and would soon get accustomed to their new quarters. When planting a fruit tree in the garden one would not use a very large specimen, as a smaller one would get established better. The same can be said of stocking the pond with fishes. Also it may be very expensive to obtain large specimens and if anything went wrong the loss would be far greater than if small, cheap fishes had been bought.

Besides fishes there are several other creatures which can be housed in the pond to make it more interesting, but care must be taken in such choice as some kinds may not be suitable. The European Terrapin, or pond tortoise is sometimes put in the pond but these creatures do not like a cold winter and could die if the pond froze over. Also they can take a bite out of a fish and so unless they are to be kept in a pond by themselves it is not recommended that they are used. Water snails are also an individual choice as their presence in the pond can be a nuisance rather than an advantage. It has often been written that water snails keep the water clear. This is a pleasant thought but in practice it is not found to be the case. Most water snails eat some of the useful water plants, they also eat food which is given to the fishes. They have a nasty habit of fouling up any dry food which has been placed on the top of the water. They soon find this and with a suction-like action of their mouths they draw much of the food towards them. If they do not eat all the food they foul the other with slime. They will also eat fishes' eggs and so are a nuisance in a breeding pond.

Some fishes eat water snails but it is usually only when they are very small, and at such times they are of little food value. Such fishes as Tench can suck snails from their shells but most fishes ignore them once their shells have become hard. A crustacean which is sometimes recommended to keep the pond water clear is the fresh water mussel, but this creature could never live for long in a newly made pond. The mussels can only move about in mud or mulm and if this is absent then the mussels would soon die and polute the water badly when they decayed. Water newts are also put in garden ponds but these amphibians only go to the water for breeding purposes and then leave the water for land for the rest of the year. They do no harm to fishes but will eat any live foods such as garden worms given to the fishes. If one wishes to breed goldfish in the pond it is possible that newt tadpoles could hatch out from the water weed and eat the goldfish fry.

The most useful fish for the pond is the goldfish. The type known as the Common Goldfish is the one usually favoured by pondkeepers. This fish is cheap to buy and looks very attractive in the pond, it is also quite hardy and can live for years in good conditions. A size of three inches over all is quite large enough for the average garden pond and such kinds can soon grow once they get accustomed to the move. The spring is the best time to introduce the fish to the water but when doing so it is wise to test the temperature of the water to see that it does not vary much from that of the carrying can or the water in which they have been kept. If the fishes are placed in a can or container this can be floated on the pond for a time so that the temperatures become more equal. Most fishes are not harmed by a slight change of temperature but it would be dangerous to drop a fish into a cold pond straight from a can of warm water.

The Common Goldfish can be bought all red or red-orange, silver or varied colours with some black. This black often goes from a young fish as it matures. There are many varieties of the Goldfish, (*Carassius auratus*), which have been bred for many years mostly in China, Japan and Korea. Some of the varieties are very handsome and an improvement on the Common Goldfish. Several are more suited to the indoor tank as they may have very large flowing finnage which would be liable to contract diseases if the fishes had to spend the winter in an outdoor pond. One of the best varieties is the Comet. This is a stream-lined goldfish with a long tail. It is a fast swimmer and moves about very well in the pond and looks most attract-ive. They may be found in gold, silver or a mixture of both.

Another very good fish for the pond is the Shubunkin. There are two types of this variety, the London, which resembles the Common Goldfish in shape but has the multi colour and the Bristol, which is a more streamlined fish with larger fins. The tail fin or caudal is much larger than the one of the London Shubunkin. Owing to the larger finnage the Bristol is not so suitable for the pond as the London, except in warmer parts of the country. The Shubunkin is one of the most colourful fishes for the pond and a good specimen should have a ground colour of a rich blue. There should also be blotches of red, brown, yellow and violet. The whole fish should be speckled with black. Many of the Shubunkins available today have not the rich blue or all the other colours but many fishes without some of the colours could very easily breed some youngsters with the desired colouring.

Another fine variety of Goldfish is the Fantail. This fish has an egg shaped body with a double tail or caudal fin. All the finnage is more developed than that of the common Goldfish but usually this fish winters well in a healthy pond. The fish may be had in a shubunkin colour or self red. The red type are scaled whilst the shubunkin type appear to have had all the hard scales scraped off. This scaleless type, found in all good shubunkins is often given the name of ' Calico ' fish.

The Veiltail goldfish although very handsome is not suitable for the garden pond all through the winter in cold districts, but makes a fine inhabitant for the furnished aquaria. The body of this fish is almost round and being so short it means that the internal organs are rather cramped. It is therefore very liable to contract swimming bladder trouble if it gets a chill. The tail fin is very large and flowing falling in graceful folds like a curtain. This fin is very prone to be attacked by a disease known as fin-rot and perhaps by Fungus.

The Oranda is another variety which resembles the Veiltail in shape but has a large protuberance over the head and gill plates which resembles a raspberry. This is known as the hood. This variety is also unsuitable for the pond for the same reasons as the Veiltail. A variety which has the hood but the body of a Fantail is the Lionhead. As this fish has less developed finnage than the former fish it could be used in the pond with advantage. A peculiar feature about this fish is that it has no dorsal fin.

There is a variety called the Moor, which is a sooty

black in colour. This fish will not show up very well in the pond but it is favoured by many aquarists. There are two types, the Veiltail Moor, shaped as for the Veiltail Goldfish and the Fantail Moor as for the Fantail goldfish. There is one outstanding feature of the Moor and that is the formation of the eyes. These are what is termed ' Telescopic '. They stand out from the head almost like a shortened form of a snail's eyes. The protruding eyes could be damaged by any sharp rock in the pond and so unless the pond is free from any projections which could cause damage it is better to leave the Moor out of the pond. If one is fancied then use the Fantail Moor in preference to the Veiltail Moor.

Another fancy goldfish which is seen occasionally in dealers' shops, is the Celestial. This fish has no dorsal fin, a double tail and eyes which have developed towards the top of the head. The eyes then gaze heavenwards, hence the name Celestial. Owing to this strange formation this variety is not very suitable for the pond as it may find difficulty if feeding among more active, normal shaped goldfish. One of the newer introductions is the Bubble-eye. This fish is rather similar to the Celestial, but the eyes have a huge bladder under them which gives them a very weird appearance. This fish is unsuitable for the pond as the bladder could be damaged quite easily in a pond. Some dealers offer a variety of Goldfish known as the Pearl scale. Most of these are of a fantail shape and so could be used in a pond but the curved scale which gives the fish its name could appear in any of the hard-scaled varieties.

Besides types of Goldfish there are other fishes which can be included with advantage to give a better variation. One of the finest for the medium and large pond is the Golden

Orfe, (*Idus idus var. orfus*). This fish is almost herring-shaped and can grow to eighteen inches in length if in a large pond. Owing to its stream-lined shape this fish is a fast swimmer and another excellent point in its favour is that it spends most of its time near the surface of the water. To see a small shoal of these fish cruising around the surface and snapping up flies is a joy to behold. Orfe have a pale golden colour but some develop black markings as they age. Orfe should never be introduced into a small pond as they require a water with a good oxygen content. In a small pond in hot or thundery weather the fish would soon be in trouble and could die through lack of oxygen. Any pond with a fountain or a water-fall would be ideal for Orfe as long as they had plenty of swimming space. There is also a Silver Orfe which, although a similarly shaped fish to the Golden is not as attractive in the water.

The Higoi Carp, (*Cyprinus carpio var. auratus*), is a large type of Carp suitable for the larger pond. It has barbels and grows quite large. It is rather slow moving but can become very tame when fed at one specific place in the pond. Some of these fish have very showy colours, almost like shubunkins in some fish. As these fish can grow over a foot long these are unsuitable for a medium or small pond.

The Mirror Carp, Prussian Carp, Crucian Carp and Common Carp are all very good fishes for the larger pond but as they all have the bronze colour they are not seen to advantage unless the water is very clear. They prefer to remain rather low down in the water except in warm weather when they may browse on the surface.

A rather recent introduction from Japan is the Nikishi-koi Carp. These fish are highly coloured and should prove valuable additions to any pond. They have the barbels of the Higoi but are more slender fishes and some are coloured more like shubunkins.

Some of the British coarse fishes are interesting and useful for the pond and the Golden Tench, (*Tinca tinca var. auratus*), is one of the best. This fish is a variety of the Green Tench, (*Tinca tinca*), and is of a soft golden colour. Both the golden and the green are splendid fishes for any pond. They are no trouble to keep and do not interfere with any other fishes in the pond. They were previously called ' Doctor fish ', but there is no evidence that their presence in a pond has any beneficial effects on other fishes. However they are very good scavengers as they will eat any large worms which fall into the pond and clear up any uneaten food left by other fishes. These fishes can also breed in the pond but must not be expected to do so until July at the earliest.

The Rudd, (*Scardinius erythrophthalmus*), is a British fish which does well in the garden pond and the golden Rudd is especially handsome when seen in small shoals near the surface of the water. This fish is much better for the pond than the Roach, (*Rutilis rutilis*), as this fish is very liable to contract Fungus disease and is so similar in the water that there is no object in introducing such fish into the pond.

The Minnow, (*Phoxinus phoxinus*) is a small fish which can be kept in a pond which is well oxygenated. As this fish inhabits running streams for preference it will do much better in a pool with a water-fall or fountain than in a stagnant one. The Chub, (*Leuciscus cephalus*), is inclined to grow too large for the medium pond and as it is rather similar in shape to the Silver Orfe, but not as likely to swim near the surface it can be dispensed with.

The same applies to the Gudgeon, (*Gobio gobia*), as this fish is a bottom feeder and is not likely to be seen very often. The Bleak, (*Alburnus lucidus*) is a river fish which prefers a flowing water and has no special claim to be included in the garden pond.

The Bream, (*Abramis brama*) is also a bottom feeding fish which is not likely to be in sight for long in the pond. It is also very darkly coloured on the back and so would not show up very well in the average pond. Sticklebacks, (*Gasterosteus aculeatus*) are not very suitable for the garden pond as they can become worrying to some of the other occupants. They are more useful for an aquarium where they may nest and breed. Another British freshwater fish is the Miller's Thumb, (*Cottus gobio*), but it is not very suitable for the garden pond as in nature it frequents rather fast, clear streams and in the pond would not thrive, remaining mostly on the bottom. The Pope or Ruffe, (*Acerina vulgaris*), is also a fish which should not be included in the pond, as it, being a relative of the Perch, could injure or eat other smaller fishes.

Two more British fishes which must never be included in the fish pond are the Pike, (*Esox esox*), and the Perch, (*Perca fluviatilis*). Both these are carnivorous and would eat any fish smaller than themselves. If it was intended to keep either of these it would have to be in a separate pond where other and smaller fishes were excluded. A small Pike, known as a Jack, could make an interesting pet as long as plenty of live foods were available. Garden worms would make a good stand-by and small fishes would be relished. The Perch is a handsome fish which could be kept where other fishes, small enough to be eaten were not included.

One fish which must not be introduced into the garden

pond is the European Catfish, (*Silurus glanis*). This fish is often recommended by dealers as a scavenger for the pond, and one would imagine that no pond could function well without one. However these fishes are carnivorous and with their huge gape could eat any fish slightly smaller than themselves. As a small specimen it might appear to be an excellent choice for the pond but when one realises that a Catfish was caught in this country not long ago which weighed 33 lbs., it can be well understood that there is no sense in putting one among goldfish etc., in the pond. As an instance of what these fishes are like I can relate having seen one which was no more than four inches long with a fully grown Stickleback stuck in its throat. What would happen to a small goldfish in a pond with such a predator can be easily imagined.

There are three newts to be found in this country which could be introduced into the pond during the spring. They are the Great Crested Newt, (*Triturus cristatus*), the Smooth Newt, (*Trituris vulgaris*) and the Palmated Newt, (*Triturus helveticus*). The first is the largest, is almost black with light coloured, tiny tubercles, and in the breeding season the male has a fine crest along its back. The second is common and the male is well coloured in the breeding season with an orange belly and a large wavy tail. The Palmate is not as common but the male can be distinguished by a thread-like filament at the end of the tail in its breeding condition and webbed hind feet.

The Newts come to the water to breed in late February or early March. Once breeding is over they leave the water and spend the rest of the year under stones by day or under thick grasses. Once these are introduced to a pond and they breed there it is almost certain that they will return the following year to breed. Any Newts hatched in the pond would also come back to breed when old enough.

Frogs and Toads can also come to the pond to breed in the early part of the year. The Common Frog, (*Rana temporaria*), can appear as early as February, and remain until spawning is finished. Also some may stay in or near the pond until the winter and remain under water in a torpid condition all the winter. The Common Toad, (*Bufo bufo*) usually comes to the pond to breed later than the frog. Neither will do much harm to the fishes but it has been known for a male frog to clasp a goldfish as it would the female frog whilst waiting for the eggs to be laid. Such a fish could be killed unless released from the clutches of the frog. It is probable that the most likely fish to be attacked would be a very sick or sluggish one. Neither appear to eat under water and so would not take food offered to the fishes. The tadpoles of the frog make a very good food for goldfish. Toad tadpoles may be eaten by fish when very small but once they get a certain size they are rejected by most fishes. The toad has a nasty secretion in its skin to deter predators and this secretion may develop in the tadpoles when they reach about half grown in size.

As has been stated before water snails can be dispensed with but if desired there are three main types which can be introduced. They are the Fresh water Winkle, (*viviparus viviparus*), The Great Pond Snail, or Freshwater Whelk, (*Limnaea stagnalis*) and the Ram's Horn Snail, (*Planorbis corneus*). The Freshwater Mussels, the Swan Mussel, (*Anodonta cygnea*), the Painter's Mussel, (*Unio pictorum*), and the species *Unio tumidus* are found in the British Isles but unless a pond has a good base of mud or mulm in which the mussels could move about, they would soon die and pollute the water. The mussels should never be placed in a newly constructed pond.

# POND MAINTENANCE

ONCE THE pond has been planted and stocked with fishes the next important factor in its well being is the feeding of the inhabitants. In any well balanced pond the fishes could probably manage quite well if left to themselves unless the pond was over-stocked with fishes. There will always be food of some kind in the water and if the fishes are hungry they will work about for it and be more healthy than if they were continually being artificially fed, when they could become lazy. Many pondkeepers are of the opinion that the fishes must be fed continuously and even when first introduced to the pond, food will be offered at once. There is no need for this as most fishes could go for long periods without food.

More fish are lost by over feeding than the reverse. Not that many fishes will over-eat but the food which is uneaten soon goes off and polutes the water. As fishes can only feed well when there is a good oxygen content in the water, it can be understood that once the water turns foul the fishes go off their food and any given just increases the danger of foul gases. Most of the kinds of fish usually kept are omnivorous, that is they eat both animal and vegetable matter. Goldfish are in this class and they can eat almost anything a pig will eat. There are many packet foods for sale at Pet shops and these can be supple-

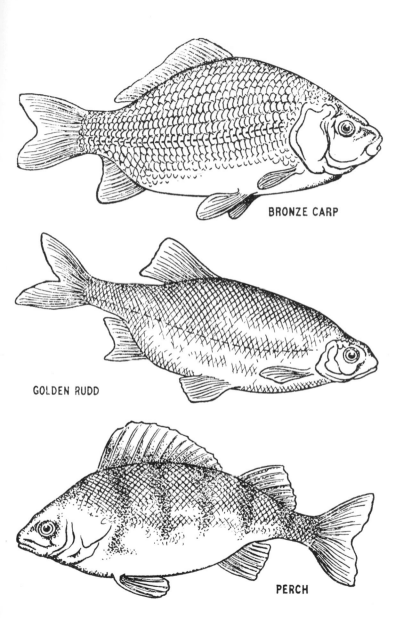

BRONZE CARP

GOLDEN RUDD

PERCH

mented by the addition of rolled oats, Bemax, dehydrated meats (as in cat foods), cheese, dry bread, especially brown; dried shrimp and biscuit. In addition some form of live food should be given every few days. One of the finest and cheapest is the garden worm. These can be broken for the smaller fishes. In addition maggots, *Tubifex* worms, *Enchytraea,* (White worms), *Daphnia,* (Water Fleas), Mosquito larvae and blood worms can be used. There are many other creatures inhabiting the natural streams and ponds which could be given but it may be found much safer to withhold from feeding some of these as they could carry disease and pests. If one keeps to live foods which have not lived in water or have been taken from wild sources, there is every chance that the fishes in the pond will remain healthy. The safest foods are those which have never been in the water and the chief ones are the garden worm, white worms and maggots.

The amount of food to be given and the frequency of feeding will depend on several factors. In the first place it must be realised that fishes are cold blooded creatures and take their temperatures from the surrounding water. When the water is very cold the whole metabolism of the fishes decreases and they would take much longer to digest their food. Once the water warms up a little the fishes become more active and need more food. However this has its limits as the warmer the water the less oxygen will it hold. It is therefore necessary to feed according to the temperature of the water. In winter hardly any need be given except in mild spells. When the temperature rises above 50 F., the fishes start to feed better and when it is at about 60-65 F., they will be feeding at their maximum.

There are small floating thermometers to be obtained which prove very useful in testing the water. In most healthy ponds the fishes could go all through the winter with no artificial feeding. Our winters are usually very changeable and while one week can be a very cold one the next can be over 50 F. One good test to look for when considering feeding the fish is to watch for their activity. If sluggish and hardly moving at all, give no food. If they are well on the move and obviously searching for food, some can be given but never give more than can be eaten in five minutes or so. Goldfish and many other similar kinds cannot eat a large meal at a time. They have very small intestines with no proper stomach. They have to eat small amounts rather often when in warm water or about to recover from spawning.

During the warmer months of the year it is possible for many forms of fish food to be present in the pond and so feeding need not be done as often, but a lot will depend on the number and sizes of the fishes and the amount of growing water plants in the pond. A medium-sized pond which was well planted could be self-supporting providing there were not too many fishes. Garden worms often fall into the pond at night and many insects will lay their eggs in or near the pond. The larvae which emerge from the eggs can provide food for the fishes. Any healthy goldfish will browse around the pond and clear up any edible matter and so the need for other scavengers will not arise. A goldfish can do all that any other scavenger could do to keep the pond water free from any matter which could cause fouling.

A good type of dried food could be mixed by anyone with the following ingredients:—Two parts rolled oats, one part Bemax, one part dehydrated meat (Cat food type), one part dried shrimp and a half part dried Daphnia or Tubifex. If kept in a close stoppered jar this food will last in good condition for a long time. When feeding only give a little to see if the fish are on the feed. A feeding ring can be used in small ponds. This is a plastic or glass ring which floats on the water and if food is placed inside it there is no tendency for it to spread all over the top of the water. If always given at the same spot it will be easy to see if it is cleared up.

Most of the fishes will benefit from the occasional feed with some form of live food. The garden worms can be encouraged to congregate if the old tea leaves are placed in one spot of the garden and a wet sack placed over them. Worms can also be collected in the garden or on a lawn by pushing a small fork into the ground and wriggling it back and forwards. This disturbs the worms which soon come to the surface for collection. They can also be caught at night with the aid of a torch, as they come to the surface then, especially on warm damp nights.

One of the best and safest foods for pond fish are white worms. These can be bred in a box of damp peat, and once a small supply is obtained from a Pet shop, they will reproduce at a fast rate if fed on brown bread which is damped. A sheet of glass must lie close on the top of the peat some worms introduced and a piece of bread put on the peat. The whole must be covered and kept in a dark, cool place. Once plenty of worms can be seen they can be collected with tweezers from the glass or by placing a small knob of cheese in a hollow in the peat. After a few days hundreds will have congregated round the cheese and they can be picked up easily for feeding to the fish. Fresh boxes can be started from the first one after a time so that worms can be taken from them in rotation.

After the pond has been functioning for a week or two it is possible that the water will take on a green hue. This is due to the formation of a green Algae. This is a free floating single-celled plant. It is an oxygenator and so it can do some good in the pond, but if it gets too thick it can spoil the look of the pond and the fishes will be lost to view. This form of Algae can float freely in the air and when it comes to rest on water quickly increases. However it cannot live without light and if any water is kept covered so that no light can penetrate it will be found that no green Algae will ever form in it. It is not possible to exclude all the light from the pond but some of it can be excluded to assist the usual water plants to keep the water clear. The Algae usually appears in a pond at the beginning of the growing season before the water plants have become strong and rampant. Once this happens much of the Algae can be choked out as it cannot compete with the strong growing plants. Also once the water lily leaves grow over much of the surface they will shade out much of the strong sunshine. Other plants such as Duck weed can be used to help to keep the water free from Algae and once it is cleared any surplus Duck weed can be removed as described in an earlier chapter.

If the water looks murky and has a bad smell it is probable that something has decayed and caused this pollution. It may be decaying vegetation, a dead fish or frog. It may be better to empty the pond and clean it out if the pond is not too large, as it is rather difficult to get a foul pond back to normal without doing so. During hot weather the pond may lose some of its water and this should be replaced with fresh. If a hose is used to run tap water into the pond it is better to use a spray nozzle so that the water is well broken up. This helps to clear out the chlorine from the water. If the water has become very green with Algae it is a good plan to change a large part of the water. It is probable that the fresh water may become green again but by the change it is possible to allow the water plants to grow stronger when they can keep the Algae down.

Another form of Algae is the filamentous type which is soft and clings to plants and the pond side; this will be eaten by many kinds of fish provided that they are not fed artificially. Should the pond get very green with Algae it is possible for it all to suddenly die off when it can pollute the water badly as it decays. Such an occurrence should warrant the cleaning out of the pond. A well balanced pond need not have the water changed at all, except once a year in the late autumn when any leaves from near-by trees or shrubs have fallen. Too many leaves left in the pond would cause pollution.

During the height of summer it may be found that some of the water plants have made so much growth that it is imperative that they should be pruned. The under water oxygenating plants are easily pruned by using a sharp knife tied on a long stick. The cut weed can then be dragged from the pond. Do not deal with all the plants at the same time but let a week go by before attending to any other kind. This will ensure that the balance of the pond is not upset. If the water lily leaves get too thick on the surface it is possible to cut off some of the older ones to make sure that a fair proportion of the water's surface is not completely covered. All the dead lily flowers should be cut off as soon as they fade or they could pollute the water.

In thundery weather, especially after a humid night it is possible for the water to become dangerous for the fishes because of lack of oxygen. Such a condition can be seen if there are a number of small bubbles on the surface in the morning or the fishes appear to be in trouble by mouthing at the top of the water. Golden Orfe are the first kind of fish to suffer from these conditions and if seen in distress it is imperative to play some fresh water directly into the pond. This usually has the desired effect unless the fishes have been left too long and have died.

During the late spring and summer it is probable that the pond may become infested with a type of weed known as blanket or flannel weed. This is a form of Algae and can become a nuisance if it is allowed to get too strong a hold in the pond. It can be introduced into the water on water plants collected from the wild or on weed from a pond which is infested. Once this weed gets a firm hold it is by no means easy to eradicate. Certain kinds of fish such as fantails can become entangled in this weed, as it catches on the tail and as the fish tries to escape by turning about the weed forms like a cord and holds the fish tighter than ever. As soon as any of the blanket weed is seen it should be removed as soon as possible before it gets too rampant. It can be pulled out by hand or a good method is to use a green stick. Break this so that the ends are rough. The stick can then be twisted among the weed when large quantities can be pulled out. Once most of this weed has been removed it is possible that the growing water plants will be able to choke the weed out or at least keep it in check.

During the year the pondkeeper may wish to add to the number of fishes in the pond. This may be done if only a few were put in the pond soon after it was made. This is the best method as it is senseless to make a new pond and stock it almost immediately with a large number of fishes before the water has matured or the plants have started to grow well. When adding any fresh fishes it is important to make sure that they are in a very healthy condition. It is a safe plan to keep the fishes in isolation, if possible, to make sure that they carry no disease or pests. When purchasing fresh specimens only buy fishes which look in good condition. The inexperienced pondkeeper may be at a loss here, but there are one or two points to look for. The fishes should be swimming about in a normal manner well down in the water, not mouthing at the surface. All fins, especially the dorsal, (back fin) should be extended, as a drooping dorsal is one of the first signs of ill health. The eyes should be bright and the whole of the fish should be clean and free from any signs of fungus. Do not always buy the largest fish as it is possible that the smaller the fish the better will it thrive when placed in the pond.

When the fish has been brought home either in a carrying can or a plastic bag, it should not be dropped straight into the pond. It may be that there is a big difference in the temperature of the water in the pond to that of the container. Before letting the fish go in the water let the container float in the pond until the temperatures are almost equal. This will prevent the possibility of giving the fish a chill.

# THE POND IN WINTER

IT IS necessary to give the garden pond special attention during the winter. Many fishes are lost in a bad spell through carelessness on the part of the pondkeeper. The most important task is to prepare the pond in the late autumn so that it has every chance of remaining in good condition all through the winter. Cold alone does not kill the fishes during a severe winter, but if the water is in any way foul when ice forms on the pond, it is almost certain that the fishes will soon be in trouble. When a coating of ice covers the water the foul gases are trapped beneath and fresh oxygen is unable to enter. The fishes are then asphyxiated through lack of oxygen and so die, not through the cold, but foul water.

Once most of the leaves have fallen from any surrounding trees or shrubs the pond should be cleaned out. If the water plants had been set in separate containers it will be easy to slide these out of the pond. The water can be emptied out by siphoning if the pond is located in a high part of the garden or the water may be removed with the aid of a small electric pump.

If the pond has been functioning for some months it is possible that there will be a large amount of mulm or mud at the bottom, together with dead leaves and decaying vegetation. This must be removed and the pond given

73

a good wash round. If the pond is a concrete one it can be given a good scrubbing round with a stiff broom. The fish should be placed in a large container during this time and before they are returned to the pond it is a good idea to examine each one to ensure that no pests are present on any of them. It is possible to clean out any medium or small pond during one day especially if the pump is started first thing in the morning.

Once the water is in a pure state it is almost certain that there will be little trouble throughout the winter. From now on great care must be taken to see that too much dried food is not given at any time. Once the temperature of the water drops below 50°F., it will be noticed that the appetites of the fishes decreased considerably. No food should then be given as long as the fishes remain fairly inactive as if any is given and not eaten within a day it is probable that the water will become foul again and so all the work in cleaning out the pond will have been wasted. During a mild spell it is probable that the fishes will take some food but this should be live food for preference. However it is possible for the fishes to go through the winter without any artificial food having to be offered.

When the pond freezes over it is very important to make sure that at least one part is kept open. The ice must never be hit as this could stun the fishes. The easiest way to make a hole is to place a watering can filled with boiling water on the ice. A neat round hole will soon be formed and the can will be prevented from falling into the water by the spout and handle. If one has electricity available it is possible to insert a heater in the water which, even if it does not prevent the whole pond from freezing over, will at least keep one part open to allow any foul gases to escape and let fresh oxygen in.

Any pond at least two feet deep should be quite safe in the winter as there is sure to be some water remaining unfrozen near the bottom. A small pond can be covered with a form of sheeting, similar to plastic glass. This does keep the water from freezing except in a very severe spell. The trouble with such a covering is that it will have to be supported by a wire frame to prevent it becoming depressed when rain collects on it. The pond should never be allowed to remain completely frozen over for more than a day and once a thaw arrives it is wise to remove as much of the ice as possible and run in some fresh water. Once the ice thaws it is possible to prick it with a stiletto-type tool when it can be broken into pieces small enough to drag out of the water.

There are many devices proposed for keeping the whole surface from freezing over, some are useful but others are not. It is said that if a rubber ball or a log of wood is placed in the water this will prevent the ice from cracking the pond. This does not function as suggested as once a fair thickness of ice forms round the ball or wood, it makes no difference to the ice a few inches away and the pressure of the ice expanding as it forms can still crack the sides of a concrete pond unless it has been constructed thickly and with reinforcement. Another method adopted by some pondkeepers is to make a strong wooden box with a lid. This is open at the bottom and placed in the pond so that the top of the box is about six inches at least above the top of the water. The box must be weighted to keep it down in the water and it can stand on bricks to keep it the desired height. The water inside the box will take much longer to freeze than that outside. Covering with sacks has been used by some people but if this shuts out too much light from the majority of the water then trouble can follow.

Should there be a heavy fall of snow on the frozen pond, it is imperative to sweep this off as soon as possible so that plenty of light can reach the water. If the pond is fairly large it may not be possible to sweep it off but it can be melted by playing the hose on it. A method adopted by some pond-keepers when ice has formed on the water is to make a small hole in the ice and withdraw some of the water so that there remains an air space between the ice and the top of the water. This is a good idea as long as there is not another severe freeze as even the water under the ice could then freeze over.

Special heaters are offered for sale by some dealers but even small ones which are used for heating a tropical fish tank can be used, as although they would be unable to make much difference to the temperature of the water as a whole they could keep at least a small hole open in the ice. Such electric heaters need only be switched on when a severe spell is expected, and they should never be used to try to warm up the rest of the water. As stated previously the cold alone will not kill the fishes but it is the bad gases trapped underneath which are the killers. Small goldfish, no more than an inch in length, can go through the winter in a garden pond providing the water remains pure.

# BREEDING FISHES IN THE POND

ONCE THE pond is functioning well and the owner has gained some experience at fishkeeping he will no doubt like to try to breed some fish in the pond. It is of course possible for the goldfish to breed in the pond in a natural manner with no special assistance from the owner. However it is better to approach the task with some special care as to ensure that success will be achieved. The easiest fishes to breed in the pond are the common goldfish. Any of the fancy varieties of goldfish could also be bred but it must be remembered that all these varieties have come from the original stock of goldfish and so can all interbreed. If fantails, shubunkins or comets are kept together they could all cross breed when the youngsters would be a very mixed lot, not worth the food they ate.

Before considering the breeding it will be useful to have some knowledge as to how goldfish function. Goldfish can breed as young as one year, as long as they had been reared under good conditions and reached about three inches long overall. It is not easy for the beginner to sex goldfish but when nearing the spawning time the males can show small, white, raised tubercles on their gill plates and perhaps on the front of the pectoral fins. The females will have a swollen body and perhaps show more swelling

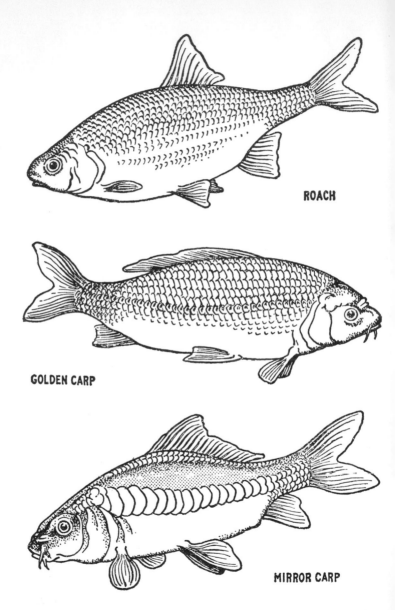

**ROACH**

**GOLDEN CARP**

**MIRROR CARP**

on one side of the body. The males are slimmer, and these
shapes are more easily examined from above.

Goldfish in a pond can breed from late April to Sep-
tember. The month of May is a very good one for spawning as this ensures that the youngsters are of a good
size before the winter. It is possible for them to breed at
monthly intervals throughout the warmer months of the
year. The fishes can be conditioned by giving them plenty
of garden worms in addition to their usual food. Any
healthy goldfish will have the urge to breed once the
temperature of the water gets up to round about 60 F.
Spawnings can be had at varied temperatures near this
but on an average over many years I have found that
60°-63° F., is the most likely one.

The female fish carries the eggs or hard roe, and the
male the milt or soft roe. When ready for spawning the
fishes will become very excited especially on the morning
of a warm or very bright day. The males will then chase
the females and nudge them about the body, forcing them
through the fine water weeds. When ready the females
expel the eggs and the males extrude their milt and the
eggs are fertilised in the water soon after they are laid.
The milt of the males contain thousands of tiny sperms
which swim about in the water around the eggs searching
for one to enter. When the eggs are first laid they resemble
tiny beads of jelly and are adhesive, sticking to any plants
with which they come in contact. They soon swell up to
the size of a pin's head. As they are transparent it is not
easy to see the eggs in the water, but if some weed is lifted
the eggs show up with a light amber colour.

The trouble with allowing the fishes to breed in a
natural manner is that once the spawning excitement is
over many of the fishes will soon make a meal of as many

of the eggs as they can find. Some of the fishes which have not been actually spawning will follow the others and eat the eggs as they are laid. If the pond contains plenty of fine-leaved under-water plants it is possible that many eggs will not be found and eaten and these can hatch out. The tale of loss is not however ended as even once the fry hatch they are still in danger of being eaten. It is probable that in many garden ponds where goldfish breed not more than one per cent of the eggs laid ever produce a sizeable youngster.

However there is no need for the pondkeeper to despair as it is possible to breed plenty of fish by the following controlled method. If one wishes to breed any special variety of fancy goldfish then it is essential that there are no other types of goldfish in the pond when breeding is expected. The breeding pond should not have too much under-water plants or many of the eggs could be lost. The ideal is a sparsely planted pond with nests of fine-leaved plants tied in bunches and anchored at the shallow end of the pond near the surface. Most fishes spawn on water weed which is either floating at or near the surface or in very shallow water. They will enter such shallow water to spawn but would never do so in normal conditions. This ensures that when the eggs are laid they will not be in as much danger of being eaten than if they were in deeper water where the fishes normally feed. Also the fish appear to know that the shallower water is usually much warmer than farther out in a pond or lake and so the eggs have a better chance of hatching out fairly quickly.

When the fish have been spawning for some time the bunch of weeds holding many eggs should be removed from the pond to a safe place for hatching. A plastic washing-up bowl is ideal for this purpose as deep containers are not required nor is it a good idea to use an all glass tank through which the sun's rays could be magnified. A fresh bunch of weed should then be placed in the shallow part of the pond and the fishes will again spawn on the fresh weed which is removed when plenty of eggs are seen.

The time the eggs take to hatch depends almost entirely on the temperature of the water in the hatching container. At 70° F., the eggs can hatch in 3½-4 days. At a lower temperature they will take longer, 8 days at 60° F., or longer if the water is cooler. A few hours before hatching the embryo can be seen in the eggs, perhaps turning over, and the eyes are plainly visible. The fry cling to the sides of the tank or the weeds and appear as tiny dark splinters. They have a yolk sac attached from which they feed for a time, again depending on the temperature of the water. As the hatching and development of the fry depends so much on warmth it is advisable to keep the tank in a warm place, either in a greenhouse or garden frame. If neither is available the tank should stand in as warm a position as can be supplied.

There is no need to feed the fry whilst they are clinging to weed but as soon as they become free swimming some fine form of live or other food must be given. The first food is usually infusoria. This is a tiny form of life which grows in polluted water and can be obtained by placing crushed lettuce leaves in a jar of water. After a few days the water will appear very cloudy and if a drop is placed under a microscope the tiny creatures will be seen moving about. Some of this water can be allowed to drip into the fry tank as food. To save the trouble of culturing infusoria there is a good liquid food on the market known as ' *Liquifry* '. A few drops of this liquid can be added to the water three times a day. As the fry grow they can be given larger types of food such as crushed white worms or garden worms. Very small water fleas can be given as soon as the fry are large enough to take them. As the fry grow it is essential that they are given more swimming space or they will not thrive. Once they are about a month old they can be given fine dried foods in addition to the small live foods.

Another method to adopt to save the eggs from being eaten in the pond is to watch for the fish to spawn and then catch a pair up carefully and transfer them to a large tank containing plenty of fine-leaved water weed. Once plenty of eggs are seen the spawners can be returned to the pond and the eggs left to hatch out in safety. Some pondkeepers place a screen between the plants in the pond containing eggs in the hope that this will prevent the parent fish from eating the eggs but once the fry hatch they can swim through the screen and be eaten in the main pond.

It is difficult to pin down what actually triggers off the spawning actions. Sometimes this can be encouraged by adding a quantity of fresh water to the pond late at night when the fish may spawn first thing in the morning. It is a fact that most fishes will only spawn when there is a good oxygen content to the water. It has been thought that the weather has some effect on the spawning times and although they may do so at the beginning of a warm spell this is not always so.

It is possible to artificially spawn goldfish by hand stripping. This can only be done when the fishes are ready for spawning. The fish is held in the hand, belly up, and slight pressure is applied from the head end of the belly to the vent. Eggs can be expelled from the female and then some milt must be extracted from a male fish in a similar manner. Undue pressure must not be used as this could injure the fish. If eggs or milt are not immediately forthcoming the fish are not ready. The fish should be held at water level with the tail under water. The gills must not be kept out of the water for more than a few minutes. After ten minutes the water can be carefully run out of the container and fresh put in. This washes away any of the male sperms which might pollute the water and encourage the formation of mildew on the eggs.

It is possible to breed some of the other species of fishes kept in the pond but as a rule this is not as easy as with goldfish. Golden Orfe will breed when about a foot long if in a fairly large pond. These fishes appreciate a well oxygenated water and are not likely to spawn in any other. A fountain or a water-fall working during the early hours of the day will often encourage the spawning act. These fish spawn in the same manner as goldfish but their eggs are slightly larger and adhere to weed or Willow roots with which they come in contact. Tench can also be bred in a medium pond. The male Tench can be distinguished by the shape of the pelvic fins. These are spoon shaped and the outer rays are much thicker than those of the female fish. Tench have bred in my pond for many years and even two year old fish have done so. When spawning these fish splash about in the shallows with considerable vigour and one would think a dog had fallen into the water. I have found that Tench spawn much later in the year than many other coldwater fishes and I have never had a spawning before July.

Rudd will also breed in a fairly large pond and these also prefer a shallow part of the pond in which to do so. Young fishes left in the pond could go all through the winter as long as they are over an inch long. Before that it is possible for the older fishes to mistake them for mosquito larvae or other creatures and eat them. The annoying part of breeding goldfish in the pond is that many of the youngsters do not change colour. The usual procedure is that when the young are about a year old they are bronze in colour similar to a common Carp. Gradually a change takes place and the lower part of the fish starts to turn pale. This paleness moves gradually up the body to the back and turns black. At the same time the lower part turns to gold. As the black on top intensifies so the gold increases until there is only a patch of black on the back. This should soon clear leaving the fish all gold. Many goldfish never change from the bronze to the gold and if such fish are left in the pond to breed it is probable that each succeeding year more fish will fail to change colour. This is one of the reasons why I recommend controlled breeding as described.

If any bronze fish are found which are believed to be over two years old, they should be removed from the pond so that they do not breed and produce many more bronze ones.

The feeding of the young goldfish which may have bred in the pond can present a problem as any food given especially for them can be eaten by the parent fish. One way to avoid this is to feed in the shallowest part of the pond into a feeding ring. The larger fishes will not swim into the very shallow water and so the young fish can get plenty to eat. If a large number of fish have been bred the over-stocking of the water must be considered. If too many are left to grow on it is possible that many will not thrive and could fail in health. It appears that no matter how well fishes are fed, if they are over-crowded they rarely thrive.

When the pond is given its late autumn clean out will be the time to check up on the numbers of fishes in the water.

Some pondkeepers think that they can get a living by breeding goldfish but this hobby should be regarded as such and no more. Even experienced aquarists cannot make a living breeding goldfish in this country as so many are imported from abroad at a very cheap price that it would not be worth while to try to do so here. A few very experienced aquarists breed some of the fancy goldfish and these can supplement their income by so doing but the percentage of very good fish bred from the finest strains is very low and even if the prize specimens command a good price many others are hardly worth the food they eat.

Goldfish for the pond could be bought for as little as a shilling each and for anyone making a start with a pond these cheap fishes are all that is necessary for a beginning. Specimen fish of fancy goldfish strains can cost as much as £5 each or more. Some of the small imported goldfish can breed the same year or the one following as long as they get good conditions. In a healthy pond they soon grow providing they have plenty of swimming space. This cannot be over emphasised as it has been found that a fish which has plenty of space but has not been artificially fed can grow quicker than fishes which are crowded, no matter how well they have been fed.

If goldfish in the pond show no attempts to spawn one or two methods can be tried. If the water does not appear to be in a very good condition some of it can be changed for fresh. Another method is to force water and air into the water with a gardening syringe. This helps to oxygenate the water and can encourage the fishes to spawn. Plenty of chopped garden worms should be given and it is a good plan to throw a piece of dried brown bread on the water during an evening. The fishes will crowd around the bread and by rubbing against one another may become excited and get the urge to spawn. I have found repeatedly that when the Tench spawn in my pond the goldfish are also encouraged to do so. When the fishes are spawning there is a distinct smell of fish mucus near the water and this may be one of the signs which start the fishes off on the breeding actions.

Some aquarists consider that it is better to have more than one male to each female as it is stated that the males encourage the female to spawn. I have found that too many males chasing the females can exhaust them too much. The milt from one male fish could fertilise the eggs from dozens of females and so it will be found that there is no necessity to have more males than females. Two year old fish seem to be right for breeding but most goldfish can continue breeding for many years providing they are in good condition.

# DISEASES AND PESTS

MOST FISHES have a protective covering of mucus which prevents the entrance of germs. When a fish is out of condition or damaged the disease known as Fungus, (*Saprolegnia*) can attack it. This appears as a woolly substance on the fins or body and if it reaches the gills proves fatal. The cure is to place the fish in a gallon of water to which is added, but not stirred, a tablespoonful of sea salt. Leave for a few days or until cured.

Velvet disease (*Oodinium*) appears as a fine, white covering of the body. The cure is as for Fungus. Fin-rot attacks the fins and causes them to disintegrate. Again the salt bath is a cure. Fin-congestion shows on the fins as blood streaks and can be caused by a chill. If fishes are purchased which have been reared under warm conditions and then placed straight into a cold pond, this trouble can follow. Keep the fish in slightly warmer water and half the amount of sea salt as recommended above until cured.

Swim Bladder trouble can be caused by a chill or can be through heredity. Fishes attacked cannot keep on an even keel, turn upside down or lie on their sides. The fish must be placed in a shallow container, a plastic washing-up bowl is ideal, and keep the water warmer until cured. Dropsy can kill goldfish and is recognised by the swelling of the body with the scales standing out unnaturally. The fish becomes very distressed. Do not mistake the natural swelling of the body of a female when in breeding condition. There is no sure cure for this disease and the best course to adopt is to kill the fish. There is no sense in trying to keep alive and breed from such a fish. The quickest way to kill a fish is to dash it smartly on a hard surface. White Spot disease rarely infests pond fishes but appears as tiny white, raised pimples on the body or fins. It is almost impossible to cure a fish in the pond and an infested one must be placed by itself in a clean tank. Try to keep the water warmer and change the fish to a sterilised tank every day. The parasites develop under the skin of a fish and when mature drop to the bottom and encyst. After a few days fresh parasites emerge and swim around until they find a fresh host. By changing the water every day the cysts are washed away before the parasites hatch out.

A few pests can attack fishes and the fish louse, *Argulus*, is one of the worst. These are like a tiny Plaice, almost transparent and no more than a quarter of an inch across. They can swim freely but attach themselves to a fish and suck its juices. They are difficult to see until a red wound is caused. If the fish is placed in a solution of a quarter teaspoon of Dettol to a gallon of water the lice will fall from the fish. Flukes sometimes attack very young fishes and the cure is as for lice. Never leave a fish in the solution for more than five minutes and remove to fresh water at once if it turns over. It will soon recover. Anchor worm, (*Lernaea*) was until recently not believed to occur in the British Isles but I have recognised this pest from specimens sent to me. It clings to a fish and can be seen as a small dark thread protruding from the body. It is actually a crustacean and not a worm. The parasite should be pulled from the fish with tweezers and the wound dabbed with Dettol.

There are a number of creatures which can inhabit pond waters. Some are harmful and others harmless. The ones which move quickly are usually more dangerous than the slower moving ones. The larvae of the Dragon flies and water beetles can attack and devour small fishes. Water boatmen can also kill very small fishes and can be recognised by what appears to be a pair of oars at their sides with which they swim. The Great Water Diving Beetle can also kill small fishes. These can fly and drop into the water at nights. The pond skaters, *Gerris*, which skim about on the surface of the pond are quite harmless. They never enter the skin on top of the water. Water lice, *Asellus*, can be good scavengers in the pond and many are eaten by fishes. They must be kept from the rearing tank as they can attack tiny fish. Fresh water Shrimps, *Gammarus*, are fairly harmless and are also eaten by fishes.

Leeches can attack a fish and could cause its death. They have to be pulled from the fish with tweezers. If there are many in the pond and cannot be caught when the pond is cleaned out, it is a good plan to tie a piece of meat to a string and lower it into the water at nights. In the morning leeches can be taken from it and destroyed. The meat should be enclosed in a loose cage of fine mesh wire netting to prevent fishes from eating it.

A very good method to adopt to catch pests in the pond is to visit it at nights with a strong torch. Many pests such as the beetles, and their larvae, the larvae of dragon flies and water boatmen, come to the surface at nights and are then easy to catch with a net. Water snails do little harm in the pond although they do little good. Their eggs may be seen on the under sides of water lily leaves as blobs of jelly. The sausage-shaped ones are from the *Limnaea stagnalis* and the roundish blobs from the *Planorbis corneus*.

Some birds can catch the fishes from a pond, the best known one is the Heron. If such a predator is to be found in the district it is a safe plan to run some strands of fine black wire around the pond about a foot from the ground. These birds usually alight near the pond and walk into it and the wire would scare them off. Kingfishers, crows and owls can also take fishes and one of the best protections is to make a wire netting cover for that part of the pond which is shallow and where the fishes can be expected to spawn. It is when the fishes are at the surface spawning that they can be so easily taken, even by cats. If the surface of the water is partially covered with water lily leaves this forms a good protection as many fishes like to lie under these and so are hidden from predators.

Providing good conditions are provided in the pond little disease or trouble will occur. Pests and diseases can be introduced into the pond with live foods caught from natural waters and water plants from the wild can also be dangerous. Such plants can be sterilised with a good strong solution of Permanganate of Potash or kept in a separate container for a time so that any eggs from harmful creatures can hatch out. Over-feeding and over-stocking can be the major causes of trouble in the pond but with common sense the pond will continue to be a very pleasant feature in any garden.

# INDEX